Saving Li'l Smokey

Written by
Adam & Celeste Deem

Illustrated by
Ryan M. Lamb

With Heartfelt Gratitude...

*To Simpson University professors Alan Rose and Dr. Brian Larsen,
your generous gift of time and expertise proved invaluable to us.
To our family and friends,
your support and encouragement sustained us throughout this journey.*

*To Tom & Cheryl Millham, Dr. Kevin Willitts
and all of the volunteers at Lake Tahoe Wildlife Care,
Li'l Smokey would never have survived without you.
"Thank You" is not nearly enough for all that you do.*

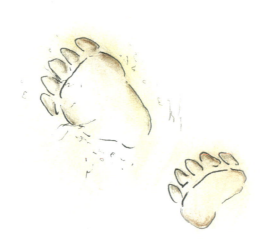

ALSO AVAILABLE IN HARDCOVER:
Visit our website at www.lilsmokey.net
Copyright ©2009 Adam & Celeste Deem
All rights reserved. No part of this publication may be reproduced, stored in a retrieval system, or transmitted in any form or by any means, electronic, mechanical, photocopying, recording, or otherwise, without prior written permission from the copyright holder, except by a reviewer, who may quote brief passages in a review.

ISBN 1440431582
EAN 13 9781440431586

In memory of our firstborn and the love of our life:
Our black Labrador Retriever
Kodiak "Kody" Thomas Deem
(2/24/1997 ~ 4/21/2010).
Gone from this earth, but never from our hearts.

Dedicated to our hero, who died saving our lives,
Our Lord and Savior Christ Jesus.
~Adam & Celeste

June 20, 2008

"CRACK!...RRRRUMBLE!" Lightning struck the forest. Thunder boomed in the mountains. A huge storm was rolling in, and this was just the beginning. Dry leaves and grass smoldered, then burst into flames. Fire crawled along the ground and into the brush and trees. "Flash...BOOM! Flash...BOOM!" Instead of rain, lightning continued to fall from the sky, more than 6,000 times. By sunrise the next morning, over 2,000 fires blazed across Northern California. In the following weeks, wildfires would destroy more than one million acres, leaving at least 300 families homeless. Thousands of wild forest animals fled their homes. Many would not survive.

July 17, 2008

"Beep, beep, beep!" Adam was jolted awake by his alarm clock. He wanted to hit the snooze button—4:30 in the morning was too early to go to work, and he was very tired. Adam had worked 27 days in a row without a single day off, but he wasn't the only one. Thousands of firefighters from all over the world worked around the clock. They had come from 41 states, and countries as far away as Greece and Australia. This was one of the worst fire seasons in California history.

Adam passed Whiskeytown Lake on his long drive up the mountain to Shoemaker Bally. He looked at the burned trees and thought about how beautiful these woods had been only weeks before. The fires had burned thousands of acres of trees and brush. Now, only charred branches and dry, brittle needles hung on blackened trees. The air was thick, hazy, and smelled like smoke. Adam drove deep into the forest.

Turning a corner, Adam spotted a tiny bear cub crossing the narrow mountain road. "Where was the mama bear?" he wondered. The cub was too young to be alone. Adam inched his truck closer and noticed that the cub was limping, stopping every few feet and lifting his paws.

The approaching truck startled the bear. He stumbled off the road and tried to climb a tree. After climbing only a few feet, he stopped on a branch and cried loudly. Even from a distance, Adam could see why— the cub's paws looked *melted*.

Adam knew that the injured bear needed help, so he radioed headquarters. Meanwhile, the frightened cub climbed down the tree and scampered down the mountainside. Adam had to act quickly, but this was a dangerous situation—the mama bear might appear and hurt Adam for getting too close to her baby. He had to do something, but what?

Adam called out in a raspy voice, mimicking the crying sounds that the bear had made only minutes before: "Nghaaaaaaaaah!" This sound caught the cub's attention, and he paused, but only for a moment. He scrambled downhill again, trying to run away. Adam figured the mama bear must not be around or she definitely would have come to rescue her baby. He hesitated anyway; should he risk getting out of his truck?

The cub was getting away! Adam took a deep breath and jumped out of his truck. Pulling cookies from his pocket, he tried to attract the fleeing bear with food, but the bear continued to run as fast as his hurt paws would allow. Adam followed him down the steep slope through the thick brush, scratching his hands on sharp branches. He continued to copy the cub's occasional cries, and although the bear was curious, he kept moving. He limped to another tree and started to climb.

As Adam moved closer, the cub climbed higher. Soon he would be out of reach! Acting quickly, Adam reached up and grabbed him by the scruff of his neck.

The little bear became all claws and teeth. Fighting and growling, he tried to bite and scratch Adam. Adam tucked him under his arm like a football to avoid getting hurt. He feared that the bear might escape his grasp and run away. "*Oh* boy . . ." Adam thought, "With all this commotion, I'm a *goner* if mama bear is anywhere nearby!"

Adam carried the bear to the truck and shuffled through his gear for something to wrap him in. Finding nothing, he held him at arm's length. With his other hand barely free, Adam called headquarters: "I have the injured cub and I'm going to try to drive out of here." The cub was howling, and the people at headquarters could only imagine what was going on. Adam wrestled the squirming cub into the truck and wondered, *"How in the world are we going to make it out of here?!"*

The dirt road was very narrow, and there was no place wide enough to turn the truck around. Adam had to drive down the mountain in *reverse*, with an angry bear in his lap! Every time he turned the steering wheel, his hand came close to needle-sharp, snapping teeth. The little bear latched onto Adam's jacket and wouldn't let go, making it almost impossible for him to drive.

Adam tried to calm the cub by talking to him in a soothing voice: "You're going to be okay now little buddy … it's alright." He could feel the cub's heart racing and feared that the bear might die from fright. How long could this wounded bear survive? Suddenly, from out of nowhere, Adam spotted a bulldozer in a huge cloud of dust. It seemed like a miracle! He stopped the truck and got out with the struggling bear tucked under his arm. Adam explained what was going on to the surprised bulldozer driver, who plowed a turnaround spot. Now they could drive *forward* and get to headquarters much faster.

Along the way, they saw more people working on the fires. George, a bulldozer operator, and Melisa, a water truck driver, were eager to help. George filled a cup and the thirsty cub desperately lapped up the water. Melisa wrapped the cub in a towel, swaddling him tightly like a newborn baby. At last he calmed down, exhausted. Melisa drove Adam and the cub the rest of the way to headquarters.

Adam stroked the little bear and spoke softly to him. "You're a good widdle bear, yes you are," Adam cooed.

During the long drive, the bear fell asleep a few times, his head drooping on Adam's leg.

At headquarters, Melisa covered the bear to shelter him from the people and noise. Adam carried him into the medical tent, where the staff was expecting a hurt person, not a bear! Despite their surprise, the medical team eagerly treated their new patient.

Adam sat with the bear on his lap while the medical team examined the cub. Melisa gave the cub a cherry lollipop, much to his delight. He tried to eat the whole thing in one bite!

For the first time, Adam felt hopeful—maybe the cub would survive. But the little bear's ordeal wasn't over. Adam gently held the cub's snout while a nurse wrapped gauze around his mouth to make sure that he wouldn't bite anyone. He didn't like that one bit, but a little later, Adam's furry new friend licked his hand through the muzzle.

The medical staff called a veterinarian, who gave them some helpful advice for treating the bear. A doctor gave him shots to help him get better. The cub growled and cried out when the needle poked him, "Ngaaah!" Adam felt terrible and scooped him back into his lap, where he hid in the towel. Then Melisa offered the cub another lollipop—a grape one this time, which quickly cheered him up.

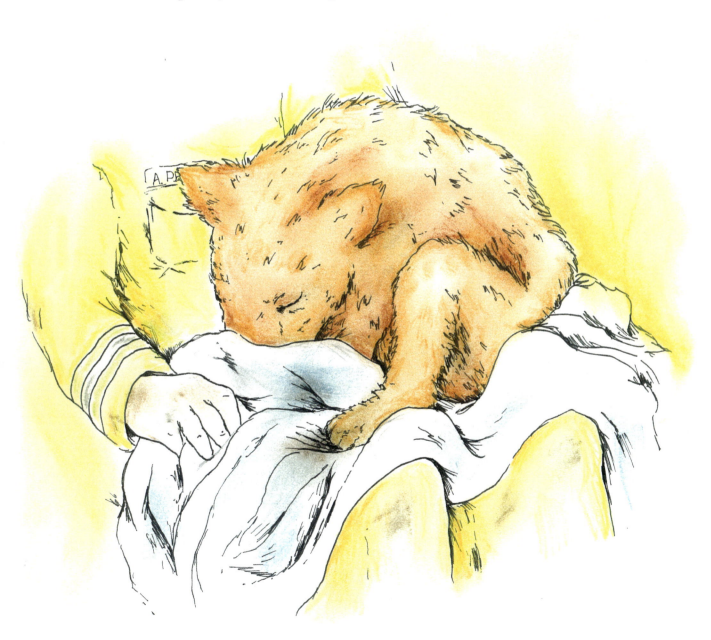

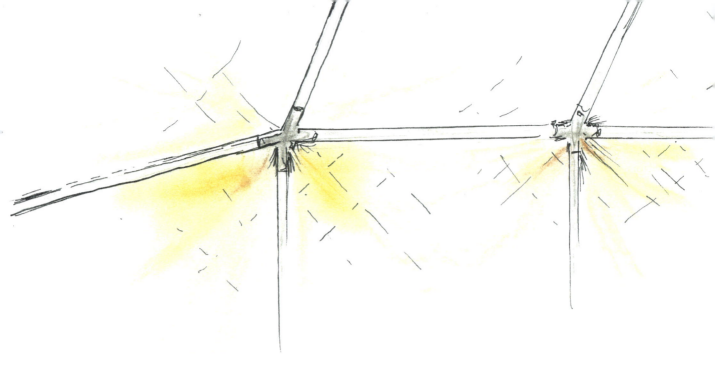

$\mathcal{F}$eeling better, the little bear playfully gnawed at the fabric knot on the end of Adam's jacket zipper. He licked the scratches on Adam's hands. He even nuzzled and "kissed" Adam's neck as if to show how grateful he was.

$\mathcal{E}$veryone in the medical tent gathered around Adam and the cub. "What are you going to name him?" they asked. Adam hadn't given much thought to naming a wild animal, so he shrugged and replied, "Maybe I should name him after the 'Moon' fire he was in, or after the area where I found him." They laughed and agreed that "Shoemaker Bally Bear" was not a fitting name for this cute little cub. Looking down at the singed baby bear wrapped up just like a little sausage, Adam suddenly knew what to call him: "Li'l Smokey" was perfect!

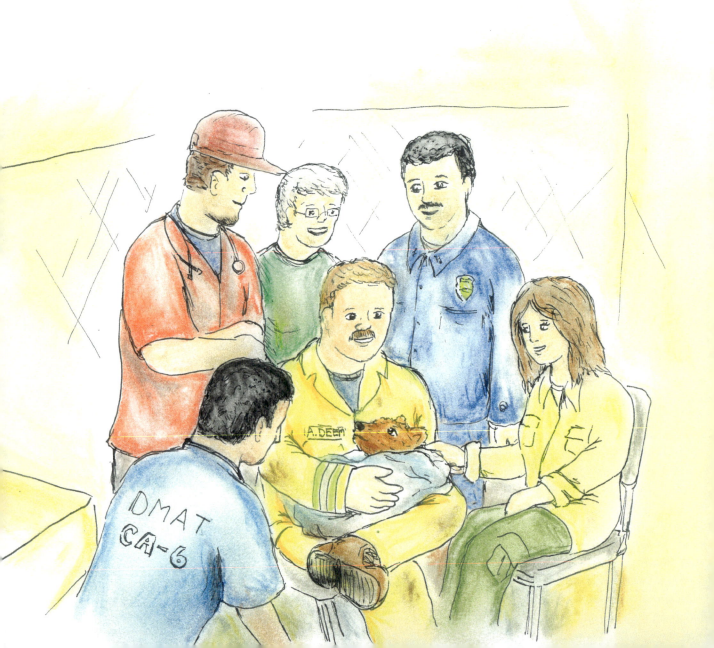

A biologist from the Department of Fish and Game arrived to take Li'l Smokey away. Adam gently placed his little friend into a pet carrier and brought him to the waiting truck. Feeling helpless and sad, Adam watched as Li'l Smokey was driven away. Where would he take the little bear? What would happen to him?

*F*ish & Game found the perfect place for Li'l Smokey—he would recover at Lake Tahoe Wildlife Care. The volunteer veterinarian and caretakers there put special medicine on his paws and tenderly wrapped them with bandages. One of the medicines they used was honey. Luckily, Li'l Smokey didn't eat through his bandages!

*H*e feasted on special milk, peach nectar, and all the food he wanted, from blueberries and wheat grass to pieces of fresh salmon.

Adam and Li'l Smokey attracted a lot of attention. Television networks, radio stations, and newspapers from all over the country interviewed Adam and called Lake Tahoe to check on Li'l Smokey. An international TV station broadcast the story throughout Europe. In a summer filled with devastating fire and smoke, Li'l Smokey's rescue and recovery seemed to lift many people's spirits.

A few days later, Adam took his wife, Celeste, to the place where he found Li'l Smokey. Walking along the rugged path, Celeste noticed something surprising in the soft, ashy dirt. "Look Adam—bear prints! And they're big!" The tracks ran back and forth between the spot where the truck had been and where Adam had plucked Li'l Smokey from the tree. Celeste wondered aloud, "Do you think these tracks could be Li'l Smokey's mom looking for him?" Just then, Adam spotted another surprise—small paw prints! Maybe Li'l Smokey had a brother or sister. Their hearts sank as they imagined a mama bear looking for her baby, but the experts had assured Adam that Li'l Smokey was so badly injured that he never would have survived in the wild.

Two weeks after the rescue, Adam drove to South Lake Tahoe to visit Li'l Smokey. He hardly recognized the "little" bear, who had almost doubled in size! Li'l Smokey did not seem to recognize Adam at all, thumping one paw against his cage in a big-bear attempt to scare Adam. Then he growled at him with a low but loud "Oooooof!" Adam was surprised, but glad in a bittersweet way. He knew Li'l Smokey was a wild animal and that he *shouldn't* like people.

Adam shared the same hope as the wonderful people taking care of Li'l Smokey—that someday he would be well enough to go back home to the forest, and maybe . . . just maybe . . . even his mom.

Afterward

Li'l Smokey received six months of intensive treatment at Lake Tahoe Wildlife Care for his second and third degree burns. He was returned to the forest on February 5, 2009, just as wild as the day he was found. He was, however, a bit bigger—Li'l Smokey had grown from eight pounds to almost 100! Before setting him free, the Department of Fish and Game attached a tag to his ear. The tag would allow them to track and check on him for up to one year. Li'l Smokey followers around the world anxiously awaited news that their favorite wild bear was safe. On April 5, 2009, Adam spoke with a biologist who had picked up Li'l Smokey's signal. Not only was he alive and well, but he was on the move, about five miles from his release site. On May 21 and September 30th, 2009, biologists again located Li'l Smokey's signal in the same general area.

Li'l Smokey was truly home, where he belonged.

*To learn more and see actual photographs and videos of Li'l Smokey, visit www.lilsmokey.net

About the Authors

Adam is a Registered Professional Forester who works for the California Department of Forestry and Fire Protection (Cal Fire). He has a Bachelor's degree in Forestry from Humboldt State University. He started firefighting when he was only 14, shadowing his mother at their local volunteer fire department in Murphys, California. Prior to joining Cal Fire, Adam started a private forestry consulting firm, Trayner Forestry. Adam lives near Redding, California, where he enjoys the outdoors with his wife Celeste and their two children, black Labrador Retrievers Lily and Murphy.

Celeste has a Bachelor's of Elementary Education from the University of Alaska Anchorage, and a Master's of Science in Counseling Psychology from Alaska Pacific University. She has worked as an elementary teacher, school counselor, and mental health therapist. Celeste grew up in Alaska, where she adopted and fell in love with her black Lab, Kody. Her avid love of nature and animals was mirrored when she met Adam while hiking in Northern California. Her motto was "Love me, love my dog," and upon meeting Adam, he immediately began tossing a stick for Kody. They were married ten months later.

About the Illustrator

Ryan's art career began with a set of finger paints at the age of three. Since then, he and his art supplies have been inseparable. Ryan lived in Seattle before moving to Redding with his family in 2004. He attended Redding School of the Arts through eighth grade and is now a freshman at Foothill High School. He enjoys many art mediums, including drawing, oil painting, and water coloring. Wherever Ryan goes, his sketchbook goes with him.

~Keep wildlife wild! Never feed or approach wild animals!~

*If you find an injured wild animal, contact the nearest wildlife rehabilitation center. To find a rehab facility, contact your local wildlife enforcement agency (e.g. Department of Fish and Game) or go to www.iwrc-online.org (The International Wildlife Rehabilitation Council).

Made in the USA
Monee, IL
02 October 2020